Fort Ardraco

An Ed Greenwood Adventure

Credits

FATEFORGE is a role-playing game designed by Studio Agate and based on the original ideas of Joëlle 'Iris' Deschamp and Nelyhann

Editorial Direction and Conception
Joëlle 'Iris' Deschamp ; Nelyhann

Editorial Coordination
Dominique 'Doudou' Lacrouts ; Joëlle 'Iris' Deschamp ; Nelyhann

Writing
Ed Greenwood

Additional Development
Clovis ; Dominique 'Doudou' Lacrouts ; Joëlle 'Iris' Deschamp

Copy Editing
Fredrik Andersson, João Bento, Kevin Dombrowski, Sara Grocott, Jeremy Loscheider, Richard Pratt, Travis Shelton, Taylor White

Artistic Direction
Nelyhann

Cover Art
Nicolas Jamme

Interior Art
Delphine 'GinL' ; Frédéric Pinson ; Olivier 'Akae' Sanfilippo ; Yvan 'Gawain' Villeneuve

Maps
Ed Greenwood ; Olivier 'Akae' Sanfilippo

Layout
Delphine 'GinL'

Studio AGATE

Based in France, Studio Agate specializes in creating imaginary worlds.
This Studio makes, among other things, roleplaying books (under the label "Agate RPG"), music albums, and video games. You can learn more and get the latest news of Studio Agate's activities at www.studio-agate.com

Agate Editions, 13 Boulevard de la République, 92250 La Garenne Colombes
Contact, questions, distribution: team@studio-agate.com

Table of Contents

Fort Ardraco

Introduction

FORT ARDRACO is intended for a party of up to 6 characters of up to 5th level. Encounters can be adjusted by increasing or decreasing the numbers of foes that the PCs will face, by lowering the damage done by those foes, and—once the PCs have reached the Keep itself—interrupting an encounter with part of the ceiling or roof falling down to scatter or crush foes, or separate them from the PCs by means of sudden heaps of rubble that block doorways.

Setting up the Adventure

When the Player Characters are either traveling to a new town or wayside inn, or returning to familiar taverns and shops after a previous adventure, they will begin to hear gossip of the following sort:

Kidnapping Rumors

"Clean gone! They found his door forced open, and a window, too! Jereth thinks it was the old 'bash the door, get in through the window, and attack him from behind while he's investigating the noise' trick. Anyway, the wizard's gone, but they left his coin and the meat in his larder and all. And on his front door that they'd broken open, someone drew a symbol in blood: a crude dragon made out of bat wings crossed by a reversed 'S' that's a barbed tail below, and a crocodile head full of fangs above."

"Kuldur taken, too? That's, what, three wizards and four clerics now, and the dragon mark drawn in blood at every place they were snatched from! What does it mean?"

If the PCs start inquiring, or if they're feasting and quaffing at an inn or tavern, they will overhear a garrulous old local (a woodcarver who was once an adventurer) telling a young and curious woman (a shopkeeper) that many local spellcasters have been kidnapped, and wherever one goes missing, a dragon symbol is found drawn in blood on a wall, post, or nearby cobblestone: two bat wings crossing a barbed tail and a many-fanged crocodile head.

This mark, the old woodcarver will explain eagerly, is a crude representation of the arms of House Ardraco, whose ruined keep stands overgrown in a forest not far away.

House Ardraco has been extinct for a century, and the castle has stood empty for some sixty summers—ever since the brigands who'd taken up residence in it were all eaten by the Horoth, a monstrous, corrupt, bloodthirsty dragon-like creature. It is "Dead Dragon Keep" now, and no one dares go near it.

For the Horoth gets hungry...

Next on the List

Regardless of how the PCs react to this gossip, from deciding to explore the ruined keep right away to ignoring it in order to pursue their own ongoing business, they will be drawn into the adventure by an ambush attack upon the PC spellcasters whenever two or more of them are in an alleyway or street—ideally a narrow one with a stretch of uninterrupted walls, so no easy exits exist.

Episode 1: Attempted Snatch & Grab

The Ambush

"Smokepots" are hurled down at either end of the alley or street, both to obscure what's happening from nearby observers and to hide the precise natures and locations of the attackers from the PCs being attacked.
Rushing through the resulting haze come brigands armed with capture-hoods and lead-weighted nets, trying to ensnare and club senseless PC spellcasters and spirit them away while disabling all other PCs. The brigands will know which PCs are spellcasters, but they will be unaware of any magic items the PCs may have, except for those used during this fight.

Special Equipment

Smokepots:

Glass or clay jars containing lamp oil, a wick, and tharrack leaves. Tharrack is a common forest and hedgerow weed with waxy, distinctively heart-shaped broad green leaves, which burn with copious thick white smoke. Once lit, smokepots are thrown to the ground to shatter, forcibly mixing the contents and causing swift smokescreens, heavily obscuring a 10-foot-square area for a few minutes or until a strong wind disperses the smoke.

Xonim's Bonds:

Xonim's bonds are magic items blessed by the Lady of the Night that leave spellcasters entirely unable to call upon their spells. This handcuff-like device is relatively common throughout Eana and is used by law enforcement to subdue or detain dangerous spellcasters. Someone might also own Xonim's bonds through serendipitous looting or outright theft. The cult owns a few of these, and they make good use of them. To bind a victim, the person must first be **restrained**, **grappled**, **paralyzed**, or **incapacitated**. Through careful coordination and honed tactics, the bandits are able to capture spellcasters, even powerful ones.

Xonim's bonds are magic items specific to Eana, and the leader is free to use them to make things harder for the PCs.

Capture-Hoods:

Eyeless "wide bags" of dark canvas with draw-cords and many grommets around their open ends, that users try to force over the heads of intended captives and rapidly pull down to below the victims' waists, constricting their arms, blinding them, and robbing them of breath. The draw-cords are then pulled tight and looped and tied through the grommets to hamper a captive so that the victim can readily be beaten senseless or controlled by means of an added neck-noose.
In game terms, this is simulated by a grapple roll. If successful, the capture-hood allows the user to inflict the **blinded** condition instead of the grappled one, which the target can escape like a normal grapple. Once the victim has been successfully blinded by a capture hood, a second successful grapple roll will inflict the **restrained** condition, and any roll from the victim to escape is then made with disadvantage.
If the victim isn't being **grappled** by an enemy, both conditions can be removed separately as an action, either by the victim or by an ally (the restrained condition must be removed first).

Weighted Nets:

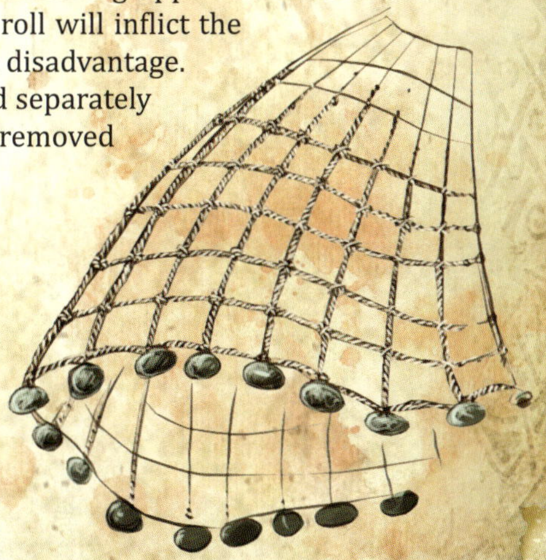

Normally employed by those hunting marsh birds or shallow-water fish, crabs, and crayfish, these nets are 12-foot-by-20-foot close-mesh knotted hemp grids with 2-pound "lead lump" weights threaded through the cords all along the outer edges. The effects are the same as a normal net, except the DC of the Strength check to get free is 8 instead of 10, due to the weighted nets not being intended for human-sized targets.

There will be 3 ambushing brigands per PC, but they will be split into two forces of roughly equal numbers, rushing from both ends of the alley or street. Each force will be led by a **thug**, while the rest of the brigands are **bandits**. The thugs are armed with maces and daggers, but will primarily use their maces and capture-hoods. As for the bandits, they are armed with scimitars and daggers, but will primarily use weighted nets, which they will toss over the PCs so that multiple brigands can tug on the net. Dragging the PCs to the ground, they will swarm over them, disarm them, and beat them senseless. The thugs will lead the charge but then step aside to watch for, and try to thwart, PCs attempting to assist each other, leaving the bandits to swarm the PCs.

The attackers are as blinded by the smoke as the PCs, but they take careful note of exactly where the PCs are when the smokebombs are thrown and rush straight to the PCs' most likely locations. They are already familiar with the terrain in the alley (puddles, uneven cobbles, debris, etc.), and have long since learned the trick of looking down for feet and ankles, because tharrack smoke rises and billows, so what's at ground level stays visible longest. The leader is free to rule that on the first round, the brigands' vision is only lightly obscured by the smokepots, as a result of their preparation.

Capture

Captured PCs will be disarmed, securely gagged, blindfolded, bound at the wrists, ankles, knees, then elbows to torso, and wrists to belts (cloth belts being provided for any PC who lacks a belt). To prevent spellcasting, their hands will be wrapped tightly in cloth bandages to bind their fingers together. The bandits will put their captives in closed, mule-drawn wagons, wrapped in blankets that leave their heads uncovered but that can be readily folded over their heads (the PCs are then considered to be **paralyzed**), and take them hastily to the Keep. PCs who struggle will have their heads banged against the wagon's boards until they stop struggling, or are stunned or knocked out cold.

Possible Conclusions

If the brigands succeed in snatching any PC spellcaster, they will hurry them via wagon into the forest, so surviving PCs will be faced with having to venture into the forest to rescue their comrades. If the brigands overcome all of the PCs, they will take them all. The leader should then let the PCs manage an escape and fight in the entry hall of the ruined keep.

It is far more likely that the PCs will prevail. The moment the fight goes against the brigands, they fling all of their capture-nets over the PCs or in heaps onto the ground in order to trammel any PCs trying to give chase, then flee, leaving their wounded and dead behind. If the PCs try to run after the brigands, squares littered with capture-nets are considered to be difficult terrain. Wounded cultists will be stricken with delirium, babbling nonsense for hours, despite any PC interrogations or spells. This is due to a drink laced with the Horoth's saliva that they have imbibed (see the Horoth's profile at the end of the scenario).

By default, captured brigands are staunch followers of the cult. As such, they wholly believe Qeldra's facade (see **Qeldra's Entrance**). Their loyalty and ignorance make it hard to get useful information out of them. However, shrewd PCs may manage to learn about the quickest way to the fort, as well as the presence of many illusions and traps. Such information may grant advantage to relevant checks, such as Wisdom (Survival) checks to navigate through the forest or Wisdom (Perception) checks to notice traps.

What if the PCs Stay Idle?

Soon after the ambush, the PCs will hear of NPC clerics (Andamarl Pureblood, Daskalan Maethur, and Orrvrin Telshield) and wizards (such as Sedmrund of the Seven Spells and Nelvarra "the Nightwitch") successfully being kidnapped and spirited away. Once more, the dragon mark was painted in blood at the scenes of these "takings."

If they elect to do nothing about these kidnappings, the PCs will soon be hired by desperate colleagues of the kidnapped clerics, who will promise generous rewards (50 gp per PC, or whatever the leader deems appropriate for their campaign), full healing, and even raise dead spells for PCs who successfully bring back their living colleagues to them. If the colleagues are dead, the rewards will be lesser.

Gathering Information

If the PCs follow up on the gossip about the kidnappings or disappearances, they will hear one or more of the following:

- A dark "dragon cult" meets at the ruined Ardraco Keep. Some of its members are seemingly innocent shopkeepers and farmers "from hereabouts," who contribute coins and dark deeds to the cult in return for aid and business enrichment. Other members are "true faithful of the way of the dragon," who have embarked on the long and painful process of being altered by surgery and magical rituals to become increasingly draconic, and who now dwell at the Keep. Most of these altered persons have scales, and a few now have fangs and claws and the beginnings of tails or snouts. If they can pass for "normal people," they will cover their alterations with gloves and clothing, but if not, they will leave the forest only by night, devouring stray animals and people when they can get them… or so the wilder claims insist. If the leader desires this adventure to become part of a longer arc, these faithful could lurk at other cult sites across the nearby countryside.
- Spellcasters who prove themselves to be particularly devoted to the cult can, by means of dark cult rituals, gain the power of dragon breath: breath weapons and fell magic unleashed in clouds from their mouths.
- Anyone who joins the dragon cult and "behaves" is rewarded for what they do, receiving gold coins from the heaped dragon hoards.
- The cult is dedicated to increasing the ranks of dragonkind and the power of the cult by gaining draconic allies and transforming willing cultists into dragons.
- Families all over the world who have draconic blood in their heritage (or believe they do) are willing spies, allies, and covert business partners with the cult.
- The cult calls itself the Eirderreth ("EAR-dare-reth"), after its founding dragon of the same name. He is said to be so ancient and so mighty in magic that he became an invisible ghost that drifts about the world, spying on and whispering threats to cult foes, guidance to cult members, and enticements to those it wants to recruit into the cult. The cult has flourished because Eirderreth keenly watches for treachery and infighting and ruthlessly eliminates those who indulge in such scheming.

The Truth of the Matter

How much of these rumors are true is entirely up to the Dungeon Master. If the cult is to become a lurking, long-term foe of the PCs, some of the "everyday townsfolk and villagers" and traveling peddlers/wagon merchants the PCs have contact with during this adventure and earlier ones could turn out to be cultists who quietly observe the PCs, judging them for later, but taking no direct part in this adventure.

What is Behind All This?

The Horoth's Purposes

The brigands have not been kidnapping spellcasters for their own benefit (though spells cast by these hapless individuals have served to improve the Keep's defenses), but rather so the Horoth can use them. Not for food, as it feeds on ordinary people and cattle or other meat brought to it, but to reproduce: sticking its tail stinger through the ears of doomed spellcasters, it plants a larval "worm" that sits in the brain of the victim, learning from their thoughts, memories, and experiences.

When it deems conditions right—that is, when the person is in a relatively safe, advantageous position of ready food and power—it begins to grow, taking control of the person's brain, and therefore of their speech. Then the rest of the body follows, the worm gorging itself and starting to transform the victim into a new Horoth. When the transformation is complete, it results in a mature specimen that will seek to keep growing in size and power until it feels secure.

The Cultists: Useful Fools

Some of the Horoth's minions sincerely believe that they belong to a famous, powerful dragon cult. After all, such practices are by no means rare in Eana, and are even common in the tropical regions under dragonborn influence. The leader can decide on the nature of the cult in this adventure, from sincere fanaticism to jaded disillusionment. What use are the cultists for the bandits and the Horoth?

- **Cash cows.** Every cultist leads a double life, shared between eerie rites and a mundane existence, hiding their commitment to the group. They must also pay a tithe to the cult, which constitutes a steady source of enrichment.
- **Informants.** All cultists are expected to tell their superiors about the presence of spellcasters and to bring back as much information as possible about them, their allies, their capabilities, etc.
- **Food.** Should the brigands lack food for the Horoth, one of the cultists is tricked into a very life-changing initiation. Those who are suspected of doubting the reality of the cult are also sometimes disposed of in such a fashion.

What Happened to the Previous Victims?

Once more, the fate of the previous victims is left to the leader.

- Looking for the kidnapped spellcasters can lead to a full-fledged campaign that will take the PCs to faraway places, starting with clues found among notes and files left in the Keep (letters, Qeldra's journal, etc.)
- However, if the leader does not want this scenario to turn into a long-term arc, they can have the PCs find the bodies in the oubliette. Despite the Horoth's efforts, all of its attempts at reproduction have failed. This can be explained by one of its victims: Nelvarra "the Nightwitch," a tiefling wizard who was favored by the goddess Xonim, the Lady of the Night. Right when she was about to be implanted with the parasite, she was able to place a curse that would make the Horoth "sterile" and doom its plans.

What Becomes of an Infected Victim?

Once the parasitic larva has settled, the spellcaster retains their skills and part of their free will for some time. The effect of the infestation on their mind is similar to that of some brain tumors: bouts of disorientation, behavioral quirks, disrupted thought patterns, headaches... In addition, any contaminated victim becomes easily manipulated by the Horoth or anyone who speaks in its name. This explains why the captive spellcasters have not offered more resistance and why they have willingly served the bandits, casting and strengthening the spells that protect their lair.

How to Get to the Bottom of This?

An easy solution would be to have the PCs find Qeldra's journal, containing all the necessary information. If the leader does not want to readily provide detailed answers to all the questions the PCs may be asking themselves, cryptic metaphors can be used to nudge them towards the next step of the adventure.

Episode 2: Ardraco Forest

Ardraco Forest is an old, thick, wild woodland crisscrossed by game trails and festooned with strangler vines and deadfall trees that have died, rotted, and collapsed. These trees' descent, however, has been stopped by their still-living brethren before they reached the ground, and they now sit wedged against them so that in every high wind they creak and groan precariously. The outer verges of the forest have some clearings where woodcutters have cut trees, but its interior is dark, tangled, and little visited, with only a few winding trails wide enough for wagons.

Popular Depiction of Fort Ardraco

At the very heart of Ardraco Forest, local legend insists, stands the brooding and deserted dark stone castle of Ardraco Keep, a small, square and intact stone fortress dominated by one soaring corner tower at its front, to the right of the door. It is surrounded by a dry moat, and its grim chambers are roamed by fearsome, hungry, predatory monsters.

This much is known by any local inhabitant, but when it comes to just what monsters, tales differ wildly, with many of the speakers swearing by (and truly believing) what they saw, though what they observed doesn't match what others have seen.

A Wild Forest

If the PCs venture into the forest, they will find the undergrowth away from the tracks and trails so heavy as to be almost impassable, full of spiky plants, clinging vines, and trees living and dead. Smaller dead trees have a nasty tendency to topple like deadfall traps on anyone trying to move past. Travel off-trail in the depths of the forest will be a noisy, exhausting process of hacking a way forward at every step, stumbling, and getting gashed by thorns and protruding tree limbs. If this noisy struggle goes on for some time, the party may face **stirge** attacks.

Lost in the Woods

Should the leader want to include a skill challenge, they can require the PCs to pass a DC 15 Wisdom (Survival) check or get lost in the forest, straying from the path and walking in circles until they can find their way again with a successful Wisdom (Survival) check (same DC).
Things can be made even more complicated and dangerous by rolling a d20 for one of the encounters below:

d20	Encounter
1-4	2 **swarms of poisonous snakes**, whose lair the PCs have just stumbled upon
5-8	A pack of 6 **wolves** led by 2 **dire wolves** on the hunt
9-12	Cult members on patrol, numbering 1 **veteran**, 1 **scout**, and 2 **thugs**. They will try to capture any spellcasters, if possible, but if things get too dangerous, they will attempt to flee to warn the others about the presence of the PCs
13-16	1 roaming **ettin**
17-20	3 **ettercaps** waiting in ambush

The game paths have a tendency to wander crazily, doubling back and crisscrossing seemingly at random. The trails are both larger and straighter, but keep looping back to meet with and cross the three winding wagon roads that converge from very different edges of Ardraco Forest to meet in front of the ruined keep. At this point, they join into one clear road that curves around thick stands of mature trees to reach the Keep itself. These trees, standing on gentle hills in the forest, hide all view of the nearby ruin from the crossroads.

The Brigands' Lookout

At this intersection, the brigands keep a lookout high up (70 feet aloft) on a platform supported by three trees growing at angles that bring them to almost touch at that height. Shifts of two men at a time (three shifts cover a day/night cycle) keep watch from a railed wooden perch concealed from observers on the ground below by fastened-on leafy, living vines.

These lookouts are **thugs** armed with daggers, scimitars, and cocked and loaded heavy crossbows, with which they'll try to shoot any PC they see casting a spell. However, their usual conduct is to remain hidden and silent while their monsters fight for them.

Unless the PCs are being particularly stealthy, no roll is necessary for the lookouts to spot them, but noticing the perch requires a passive Perception of 16, due to how obscured it is. The thugs are stationed here to discourage all non-cultists from approaching Ardraco Keep by unleashing captive monsters from cages. The lookouts do this by pulling on cables that run up through holes in their platform and are held in place against its floor by large, wooden toggles or crossbars too large to fit down the holes, so the lines can't drop through and be lost. Two cables can be yanked on to open two separate cages, and it takes little effort to do so, thanks to pulleys that take the weight off the long ascending lines.

The Lookouts' Watch Monsters

An Old Manticore

One cable lifts the front "gate" of an old and rusty, but massive and still very sturdy iron-barred cage behind the first hill, at the curve of the trail running on to the Keep. The cage holds an aging **manticore**, weak from lack of food and old wounds. It only has 44 hit points, its wings have been clipped (it can't fly), and it has only 3 tail spikes left, amid stubs that will become new spikes 3 days from now—its spike regeneration is very slow these days. It has been trained to head for the bend in the trail in search of both food and revenge, goaded on many occasions by cultists who jabbed it repeatedly with blunt spears, only to retreat around the bend toward the crossroads. When unleashed, it will prowl like a lion in that direction, seeking to slay and devour anyone it sees.

A Ravenous Owlbear

The second cable the lookouts will pull opens the iron-barred lid of a pit-cage right behind the lookouts' trio of trees. The cage, covered with earth and growing forest plants, and pierced by several hollow, dead "breathing tube" tree trunks, is not immediately visible, but as soon as it is opened, a starved and tormented **owlbear** will swiftly climb out of the pit and attack anyone it can reach.

Attacking the Lookouts

The owlbear's targets probably won't include the lookouts, because they ascend to their platform up a ladder of wooden rungs nailed on one of the trees that support the platform. For much of the upper "run" the trees are too close together for any owlbear or other Large creature to fit between their trunks. This also serves as a safety measure, since a climbing lookout who slips will usually slam into the tree behind them, skid down it, and be able to grab another rung before falling all the way to the ground. Moreover, a twenty-foot stretch of all three tree trunks immediately below the platform lacks rungs and has been fitted with leather collars that have been coated inside and out with extremely slippery (but not all that flammable) leaf oils. The lookouts can readily cut the straps holding the collars closed, because their ends are brought up and over some boards of the platform. Cut collars will plummet to the ground below, and anyone climbing them must make a DC 13 Dexterity saving throw to recover, or fall for 6d6 bludgeoning damage.

The only way up or down past the collars is with the assistance of climbing-ropes let down from the platform. If the lookouts see non-cultists climbing, they'll either pull these ropes up, or not let them down in the first place. In any event, they will have plenty of opportunities to let loose crossbow bolts into the faces of climbers trying to get past the slickly oiled collars. Due to how easy it is to hit someone climbing up the ladder right below them, their attacks are made with advantage.

Raising the Alarm

The lookouts also have war horns they can blow to alert anyone in the ruins of the approach of "hostiles" (double blasts) or that they've had to unleash the guardian monsters (triple toots). They can also signal cultists in the ruins to unleash the backup monsters with a very long blast, or the hurling off the platform of a crash box (a barrel full of old, useless rusty scraps of armor and weaponry and shards of broken glass, which will land with a loud and spectacular crash).

Last Resort: Giant Spiders

This is a desperation tactic used only when large numbers of foes show up, or when determined intruders have penetrated the ruins and are departing again. In the latter case, the leader should decide whether or not any cultists are in a position to set loose these backups, or want to. The reason why these are a last resort is that they are as much of a danger to the cultists as to the PCs.

These backups are three **giant spiders**, all caged separately in vine-cloaked, close-grid iron-barred cages affixed to the backs of trees right beside all the trails, one cage on each trail, just before the trails come together at their intersection.

Each of these angry, hungry giant spiders will block the PCs' way home along "its" trail. The cultists will probably watch from hiding and only unleash a spider to block the trail chosen by the PCs, but of course, if the PCs elect to retreat from a spider to the crossroads and choose another route, eventually two or all three spiders will be loosed to hunt.

Episode 3: The Gatehouse

Once the PCs have overcome the lookouts and their guardian monsters, they'll discover that Ardraco Keep isn't the intact fortress that local legend claims it to be. It has long since burned and collapsed into a roofless ruin all but completely reclaimed by the wild forest—at least at ground level.

Getting Inside

The dry moat does exist and consists of a precipitously deep ditch, about forty feet wide and twice as deep, with jagged rocks waiting at the bottom: over the years, rainwater has filled much of it with slimy mud and stagnant standing water. The one way across this formidable moat is a still sturdy, narrow, rail-less stone bridge, starting from a stone gatehouse in the forest and ending through the gaping entry arch of the Keep proper. The castle's front wall is intact, though the huge tower that once dominated the landscape has long since collapsed into a tumbled heap of now-overgrown stone blocks and rubble.

The gatehouse has deliberately been constructed to block all access past it, unless the PCs are able to bypass it entirely. They could accomplish this by, for example, very skillfully throwing a grappling hook and line across the bridge at an acute angle, then somehow retrieving its far end to gain enough tension to use the line to gain access to the bridge, or firing a heavy crossbow bolt to drag a line behind it. The right spells can also accomplish this, but not dealing with what's in the gatehouse leaves it as a problem to be dealt with on the way out, when things might possibly be more hectic than when the PCs are controlling their own rate and means of approach on the way in.

The bridge itself is solid and massive: a single huge bar of stone, chiseled flat and smooth on its top but rough, rounded and jagged on the underside. It looks like it was carried here as a single slab and laid in place on now-buried stone sills by a giant (and that's exactly what happened).

The gatehouse must have looked grand once. Although only about fifty feet square, it had very thick walls of fitted stone blocks, a soaring, tiled spire, and open archways at both ends high and wide enough for the grandest coaches, guarded by massive portcullises.

The spire is now an open, gaping stub, its tiles fallen everywhere the eye can see. Both the inner and the outer portcullis fell down into place to block the way, and then rusted there, dwindling to mere forlorn remnants years ago.

A Castle of Illusions

As the PCs see the gatehouse, it is clear that the way across the bridge is navigable. It passes through a matching archway in the front castle wall, whose massive ironclad wooden doors have had their own collapse and fall. It is also clear that magic has been cast in the gatehouse: weird, shifting "fuzzy gray glows" flow and surge endlessly inside, blocking any clear view of what's within, though every PC gets the impression that fairly large creatures are milling about, in eerie and utter silence.

If any PC casts any sort of magic at the gatehouse, the gray glows will fade. They were obviously some sort of barrier or shell, because as they fade, six **minotaurs** will be revealed, greataxes in hand as they charge straight out of the gatehouse at the PCs, shaking the ground with their hooves but still eerily silent.

In truth, these are stolen cattle, magically penned up in the gatehouse; cult spellcasters cast illusions on them to make them look like minotaurs, and spells keep them silent and induce them to charge. If PCs don't get out of the way and instead try to stand and fight, they'll get trampled, which can be treated as the Trampling Charge of a **warhorse**. If the PCs just step aside, however, the "minotaurs" will rush onwards along the wagon trail, the illusions on them fading to reveal their true nature as farmyard cows. Their magical goading and the magical silence both fade with their disguises, so within view of the PCs, they'll become cows, bellowing, sweating and lurching to a rather bewildered halt.

This ruse is intended to waste PC spells and identify spellcasters to cultists watching from hiding. There is nothing in the gatehouse of interest except a lone metal bucket that miraculously escaped rusting and is intact and watertight, with a sturdy metal handle that still swivels.

From this point on, as they explore the ground level of the Keep, all the creatures that the PCs encounter are magically disguised. The brigands all look like animated human skeletons, and the monsters appear as different creatures. These illusions fade, blow by blow, during combat, but return slowly when there are breaks in combat. When a creature is slain, the illusion on it vanishes for good. Creatures in the underground areas of the Keep appear as themselves.

Where Do All the Protective Magics Come From?

With a successful DC 15 Intelligence (Arcana) check, the PCs will notice that the illusions that manifest here are particularly powerful, far-reaching, and durable. The illusions work similarly to the *seeming* spell. The anomalies can be caused either by the location's nature or by the presence of an artifact. The leader is free to pick whichever option best suits the campaign. One will provide convenient plot hooks, while the other will be more restricted to this scenario only.

Artifact: The Orb of Illusions

In the past, Qeldra raided a Traveler ruin along with other adventurers, whom she later betrayed and abandoned to certain death, taking the Orb of Illusions with her.

This unique magic item contains 10 sorcery points and grants a rare and forgotten metamagic effect: "Lunar spell." When casting a spell with a duration of 1 minute or more, the caster can spend 1 sorcery point from the orb to extend the duration to the equivalent of a lunar cycle of Melancholia.

Qeldra has studied the lunar orb, and constructing the Keep's defenses has allowed her to familiarize herself with its powers. Unfortunately for her, the Melancholia-infused magic comes at the price of the user's sanity, and she has slowly been losing her grip on reality.

Where does the Orb of Illusions come from? Who financed the expedition Qeldra was part of? What if her former boss sent agents after her, seeking to recover the powerful artifact?

Geomagic

On Eana, magic currents are variable. Some regions are powerfully charged magically, others less so. The variations can be more or less sudden, extensive, or localized. They can also have different effects depending on the school of magic. In the present case, the Keep's spellcasters have noticed that, through specific rituals, illusion spells can easily be made more powerful and lasting.

If the leader so wishes, they can let the PCs use their enemies' own weapons against them, through the casting of illusions of their own. Spellcasters can learn about the ritual by examining remains in the castle's entry hall. So that the PCs can actually cast the ritual, its material components should be something like nettle leaves or bramble thorns—something they can easily get their hands on before confronting the cult for good.

When an illusion spell is cast with the additional material component, it becomes more powerful, receiving one or two bonuses at the leader's discretion: increased number of targets or duration, longer range, twinned spell, etc. If the PCs are a bit out of their league, this serendipitous advantage can give them the necessary edge to prevail.

The Entry Hall

As the PCs approach the gaping front archway, all is quiet and dark within. Scorch marks along the upper reaches of the crenelated stone front wall of Ardraco Keep indicate that a fierce fire raged along its roofs a long time ago. The wall rises about as high as a four story building. Creeper vines have colonized it here and there, growing as thick as trees and cloaking it in heavy greenery. All seems peaceful.

As with the portcullis of the gatehouse, all that remains of the portcullis that long ago fell to block the entry arch is a few vertical rusty stubs of iron bar, high above the PCs' heads, that will fall into red dust and flakes if touched. They can't be salvaged for use as weapons or tools.

Beyond the 20-foot-wide archway is a large, roofless rectangular chamber. This entry hall is 60 feet across and 80 feet deep, its floor of weathered flagstones heaved and cracked by winter frost; saplings, weeds, and bushes sprout here and there in the cracks where stones meet.

The room, which is dominated by a central, newer-looking 20-foot-tall stone statue of a dragon-headed man, is empty of living creatures when the PCs first see it. In each rear corner is a large, closed treasure chest, hoop-topped and bound in metal straps; the type known in legends as "pirate treasure chests." Each about 4 feet tall and wide and 6 feet long, big enough to hold two human bodies.

Spaced across its rear wall are three closed, solid-looking, ten-foot-wide wooden doors.

The stink of death is strong, for recently-killed, rotting corpses are sprawled here, clad in leather armor but lacking weapons, helms, or shields; even their purses and belts have been taken. Six dead humanoids, possibly adventurers, disloyal brigands, or just curious woodcutters, lie scattered across the room, all of them stabbed and hacked by edged weapons. Flies, crows, vultures, rats, and other small forest creatures have been at them; their eyes are missing, and much of their ribcages have been torn open and devoured.

The statue at the center of the roofless hall is finely carved out of soft grey stone, in the likeness of an open-mouthed, dragon-headed man, arms outstretched and fingers spread. It is immobile and remains so, but will speak to the PCs… thanks to a speaking tube running from the back of its mouth down through its body, to a cultist in the dark Large Cellar beneath the Entry Hall, who can see up into the entry hall through more than a dozen tiny spyholes hidden in the seams between Entry Hall floor flagstones.

The Talking Statue

As PCs first enter the room, the statue will speak in a loud, imperious voice, asking, "Who are you, who approach the Dragon God? What is your purpose here?"

It will thereafter engage in discussion with the PCs, trying to learn all that they will let slip about their names, professions, abilities, magic, and intentions. The voice won't admit that it's a human and will pose as "an immortal servant of the Dragon God," claiming that it has itself no name, but is empowered by the "unseen, all powerful divine dragon Eirderreth, who leads and inspires us all."

The statue falsely claims to welcome allies of the cult (which it will call "the faithful of Eirderreth"), and those aspiring to join the cult. In actuality, true allies and applicants are received elsewhere, and invited to the Keep only after winning trust by dedicated service to the cult and after being investigated. It will invite PCs claiming to be believers to "go through the center door, proceed to the back of that room, leave your weapons on the table with those already surrendered by others, and pass through the door beyond, to meet Sister Amrathra, who will welcome you to the Dragon."

The statue will instruct the PCs not to "open or even approach" the chests or the other doors and will attack if they start to vandalize anything, including the statue. If the PCs reply rudely to, defy, or ignore the statue, or cast magic in the room, the statue will also attack. Examining or even removing the corpses will not be considered vandalism, and if questioned about them, the statue will say that the bodies are those of "unbelievers being returned to nature, as is only fitting."

The leader should, without being blunt or obvious about it, try to establish where each PC is once the statue attacks begin: is everyone inside the Entry Hall? Where are they standing? This matters once the Crossbow Attack (see the next page) begins.

The Statue's Enchantments

The statue has a special "gem" (actually a faceted lump of enchanted rock crystal) set inside its head that is magically linked to anyone bearing a matching crystal stone—in this case, the cultist in the cellar below.

It enables anyone who triggers a wand or rod touching that matching stone to unleash the powers of that item through the linked gems, so the wand's powers issue from an eye or mouth of the dragon-headed statue. To get the rock crystal, the PCs will have to crack open the head of the statue without shattering this "gem," which is, by itself, worth 50gp.

In addition, the statue has also been enchanted so that any voice coming out of it sounds like the thunderous one of a dragon. This has the added benefit of concealing the cultist below more effectively.

Combat in the Entry Hall

The Statue's Combat Tactics

Once combat has begun, the cultist will make the following statue wand attacks:

- **First round**: One fifth-level *magic missile* spell (7 bolts, each dealing 1d4+1 force damage) from a *wand of magic missiles* having 7 charges.
- **Second round**: One *polymorph* spell from a *wand of polymorph* having only 1 charge (Wisdom save DC 15). The cultist will attempt to turn a PC into a beetle, targeting apparent spellcasters or aggressive PCs over other combatants.
- **Third round**: One second-level *magic missile* spell (4 bolts, each dealing 1d4+1 force damage) from the same *wand of magic missiles*, exhausting it.
- **Fourth round**: An attack from a *wand of wonder* having 1 charge on a lone PC, who is automatically affected (no save to avoid). The PC's skin turns bright blue for 1d10 days.

The cultist will break off the attack if the PCs plead or try to bargain, but will renew his magic assaults if they turn hostile again. He will maintain a calm manner throughout, and fall silent once the statue's possible attacks are exhausted, but will signal to colleagues in adjacent cellars to initiate the Crossbow Attack with a briefly unhooded lit lantern, which the PCs can notice with a passive Perception of 16.

The Crossbow Attack:

Six **thugs** among the cultists, all armed with heavy crossbows, as well as maces and daggers, attack in unison. Two of them will appear through the center (guardroom) door in the back wall of the entry hall. One opens the door so the other can fire, then the opener scoops up his cocked and loaded crossbow and fires while the other manages the door; after both have fired, they slam the door and rush to the guardroom's trapdoor and depart through it, so PCs racing after them may discover the guardroom deserted.

The fight can be made tougher by the intervention of additional brigands. They could be back from patrolling the forest, hunting for food, or spring from remarkably well-hidden passageways.

The other four thugs come through the gatehouse. If any PCs are still outside the castle, they fire across the bridge at those PCs, and through the entry arch at any PCs visible in the entry hall beyond. If all of the PCs have entered the castle, they rush to the entry arch and fire into the entry hall to attack the PCs from behind, then flee back into the forest again. If any caged monsters in the forest weren't unleashed earlier, PCs in pursuit will face them now.

All of these attacks are ranged weapon attacks, +2 to hit, range 100/400 feet, dealing (5) 1d10 piercing damage. This is a single, "hit and run" volley, so unless the PCs are visibly badly wounded, none of these attackers will tarry to fight.

The Ultimate Attack

The cultist controlling the statue from the Large Cellar isn't alone. Moving around the cellar from spyhole to spyhole, and so being able to partially or wholly avoid most magic cast down through the spyholes, is a second cultist. This accomplice takes no part in any fighting or statue speaking, but concentrates on studying the PCs. When he deems the time right, he will open the doors into the east and west staterooms by means of separate pull-cables down in the Large Cellar. Doing so will release the monsters in those rooms into the entry hall to attack the PCs. This will usually be after the Crossbow Attack. With a passive Perception of 16 (17 if they are in the middle of fighting or otherwise doing something noisy), the PCs will hear the cultists shuffling in the cellar below.

The two treasure chests in the entry hall are closed and locked. When the locks are picked, there are loud "clack" sounds as traps that formerly shot out poisoned darts go off harmlessly. One trap shoots a blunt-tipped practice dart that will hit a PC but do no damage. To it is attached a scrap of cloth bearing the message: "You Are Doomed." The chests are empty, placed here by the cultists as lures to draw intruders to where they can be attacked by monsters unleashed from the staterooms.

Deeper Into the Keep

The three doors across the back wall of the entry hall all look identical. They are all ten feet wide and tall and are all unlocked, hinged on the left side of someone facing them from the entry hall, and swinging away/inward into the spaces beyond them. The center door leads into a guardroom, and the doors on either side of it lead into staterooms.

The Guardroom

This 20-foot-wide by 40-foot-long room has an intact ceiling and stone walls. It also has a closed door in the center of its far/back wall, and against the back wall just to the left of that door is a stout, crude wooden log-and-board table with three gleaming, polished scimitars lying on it. These scimitars are real, sharp, magnificent-looking and non-magical. They are each worth 50 gp due to their superior craftsmanship.

The rear door of the guardroom opens out onto a wild forest vista of overgrown castle ruins; nothing of the Keep survives at or above ground level, except the dry moat ahead.

The entire ceiling of the guardroom is actually a trap. It is made up of horizontal wooden doors with stone masonry mortared to them so as to look like a stone ceiling. Weighted by the stones, the doors are heavy, and hang from ropes run through overhead pulleys attached to crossbeams erected by the cultists. They are connected to pressure plates in the guardroom floor via cavities in the walls dividing the guardroom from adjacent staterooms.

These pressure plates are large flagstones that sink a few inches when stepped on, triggering release catches for the ropes and causing all of the doors to fall. This will bring down the entire "ceiling," on the room, except on the back corner where the bench with the scimitars is. The pressure plates can be spotted with a successful DC 15 Intelligence (Investigation) check. Sixty pounds of weight is needed to depress a plate. As such, one of the entry hall chests isn't heavy enough, but both of them landing near each other would reach the required weight.

The first 10-foot section of the floor (just inside the door from the entry hall, from side to side across the guardroom) is "safe": its stones are solid, not pressure plates. However, if the falling ceiling is triggered, anyone in this area will still be caught in the area of effect. There is a secret trapdoor in the floor at the west end of this "safe" strip, allowing access to the Large Cellar room below. Finding this trapdoor requires a DC 20 Intelligence (Investigation) check.

The DC for the Dexterity saving throw to get back out of the guardroom and avoid being hit by the falling ceiling is 11, but is only available to PCs whose position makes this possible; otherwise, they get slammed to the floor by the falling doors and suffer 3d10 bludgeoning damage.

West Stateroom

This 20-foot-wide by 40-foot-long room with stone walls has an intact ceiling and a closed wooden door in the center of its back wall. It contains a beast that looks like "a powerful lion—four clawed legs and a tail—attached to a beautiful feminine human-like upper body, with human arms and head and flashing eyes." However, this is a magical illusion of a lamia; underneath this seeming is really a hell hound that will breathe fire at the PCs as soon as the door is opened. If the PCs slam the door, the **hell hound** will hurl itself against it repeatedly, but will have to batter it for a very long time to force its way through. The room is otherwise empty; the door at the back leads out of what remains of the castle into utter ruins, choked by growing forest. The same vista is reached by the adjacent rear guardroom door.

East Stateroom

This 20-foot-wide by 40-foot-long room with stone walls has an intact ceiling and a closed wooden door in the center of its back wall. It contains a beast that looks like a "dark-blue, many-finned, scaled and malevolently-glaring creature with two arms ending in taloned human-like hands, a long powerful tail, four barbels writhing about its fanged mouth—that is swimming in the air!"

This is a magical illusion of a merrow; underneath this false guise is really a **minotaur** (yes, unlike the false minotaurs in the gatehouse, this one is real) that will charge the PCs once the door is opened, swinging its greataxe and goring them. It has been put into a magic sleep that ends when the door is opened, and is quite capable of wrenching open the door and pursuing the PCs anywhere.

The room is otherwise empty. The door at the back leads into the Feasting Hall, which is the way forward for PCs seeking to go deeper into Dead Dragon Keep.

Feasting Hall

This roofless, windowless room has soaring stone walls that rise 70 feet into the sky. It is a rectangle 50 feet wide and 120 feet long, with the door from the East Stateroom in the westernmost ten feet of its 50-foot-long south wall, a dark, 6-foot-wide archway in its east wall right beside where the east wall meets the south wall, and a closed, 6-foot-wide wooden door in the center of its back/north wall. The room is full of 14 "skeletal horses." These are actually illusions cloaking fourteen stolen cows, all standing placidly, swishing their tails and looking up to regard the PCs. They stand amidst copious heaps of their—slippery!—dung, and bales of hay for them to eat.

These "dangerous monsters" are chewing their cud, and will snort and low occasionally if left alone. If they are attacked, they will bellow and kick and try to flee, shoving each other as they hasten to the far end of the room. If pressed, they will become panicked, and will charge PCs, lashing out with their hooves and trampling those nearby.

These beasts are the brigands' larder. Treat them as **draft horses** if fought.

The archway in the east wall leads to a 6-foot-square alcove, too narrow for any cow to do more than poke its head into. Inside is an enclosed spiral stone staircase descending 70 feet down into dank, chill, earth-smelling, stone-lined surroundings: the subterranean level of the castle. Going down, the PCs will reach the Ritual Room.

As for the back door of the Feasting Hall room, it opens into a ruined, blood-drenched Kitchen.

Kitchen

This 30-foot-wide, 50-foot-long room is roofless and ruined, with many gaps in its stone walls where past fires have caused collapses. Everything is drenched with blood, both months-old black stains and recent, dull red, sticky smears. The reek of death is strong, and flies buzz everywhere. There are 6-foot-wide doors in the center of its north and south walls, and a wider door in the center of its west wall is part of the largest gap. To the south of this kitchen is the feasting hall. On its other three sides, the kitchen, formerly flanked by various wooden pantry wings and additions, is now surrounded by wild, growing forest that has reclaimed the aboveground Keep ruins. In three spots amidst this tangle of saplings, vines, and brush, there are blackened areas where large fires have in the past been kindled, and a set of iron tripods supporting a massive spit stands in one of these improvised hearths.

In the center of the stone floor is a four-foot-square stone block with a massive, rusty—but still sturdy—iron ring set in it that has a 12-foot-long felled tree "handle" thrust through it, so that two strong persons taking either end can readily lift the block away. If this is done, a dark shaft down into the darkness below is revealed, at least forty feet deep and probably more (it is 60 feet, and descends into the Deep Cellar, where the Horoth awaits.)

Here the brigands of the cult have been butchering cattle taken from the feasting hall, which they then cook on one of the outdoor hearths for their own consumption—or lower in raw and dripping chunks down through the trapdoor to the Horoth in its lair below.

Dungeon Level

Ritual Room

This impressive, 70-foot-square cellar room with a 20-foot-high ceiling is fashioned of stone painted matte black, its walls and ceiling coated in melted and fused black glass for a smooth, glossy appearance.

The room is dominated by a human-sized waist-high black wooden table or altar six feet square, with black wooden posts at its four corners that jut up another two feet higher and are capped with the preserved claws of dragons, talons open. The rest of each post is covered with overlapping dragon scales down to the floor, and floor-length black skirting is affixed around the edges of the table.

The tabletop is covered with an uneven accumulation of melted and re-hardened black candle wax, from where hundreds of fat, round, black candles have been set here and burned down, over time outlining an X-shaped clear area where a human body has lain spread-eagled.

Across the entire northern end of the room, four feet out from the wall, hang thick, heavy floor-to-ceiling black canvas curtains, in ten-foot-wide overlapping strips. That way, there are many places someone can push through them while still allowing a clear path along the wall behind them. Additionally, they are too heavy to billow or otherwise move in response to someone walking along behind them who doesn't actually brush against them.

The Magics of the Chapel

This Dragon Cult Chapel is a sham intended to impress the gullible, helping to recruit people to serve the cult as allies, suppliers, and spies. In truth, there is no dragon cult, just brigands who serve the monster known as a "Horoth" for mutual benefit (see the Horoth's profile at the end of the scenario). However, this chapel has been crafted—and improved upon by various captive spellcasters over the preceding months—to strongly suggest otherwise. A *grand warding* (a long-lasting, persistent variant of the *guards and wards* spell) has been cast here that makes the entire area radiate magic, and also has the following properties:

- Only spells cast by the *grand warding*'s caster and any other creature designated during the casting have their normal effect. All other spells are absorbed by the *grand warding* to extend its duration, which is already 1 month long by the time the PCs first enter the Keep.
- The illusion of an eight-foot-long dragon's head (on a neck that seems at least three times that length) "fades into view" in the air above the altar table, as if it is nosing down through the ceiling and cocking its head to regard everyone in the room. It is purple-and-black-scaled, fanged, long-snouted, with gold-and-black eyes, and two forward-thrusting horns. However, it is not a dragon of any precise type or species that the PCs will recognize. It is silent and does not react to PC actions unless something solid impinges on the area in which it is manifesting, in which case it will shake its head sadly and withdraw, fading away again. If not so interrupted, it will peer around the room from above the altar table, nod slightly, and withdraw, fading into invisibility as it does so.
- A *magic mouth* has been placed on the underside of the altar table, hidden by the skirting. If any PC touches any part of the altar, it will say in a loud, deep, rumbling voice "You stand within the shadow of the Great Dragon! Worship me, and prosper! Defy me, and perish!"
- A *magic mouth* has been placed on the north wall of the room, concealed behind the black curtains. If anyone approaches within 4 feet of any part of the curtains, it will say coldly, "Proceed closer, and die horribly. You profane the Great Dragon!"
- All of the traps in this room (see the next page) are concealed by the *grand warding*. They can't be detected beforehand except by deliberate actions stated aloud by the players, like bashing an area of floor with a weapon or item. Thus, attempts to detect or disable a trap cannot be "I'm going to check for traps" dice rolls, but must be specifically stated PC activities, such as "I'm going to toss my shield onto the floor in front of me to see if anything happens." The leader may let the players know of this.

As designated during its casting, Qeldra is unaffected by this *grand warding*; she sees through its illusions, her spells are unaffected by it, and her activities don't trigger any of its actions.

The Traps

The traps in the room are as follows, with letters referring to locations marked on the map:

A. Spring Darts: The area of floor here is a pressure plate that goes down, revealing spring-loaded launchers that flash out and shoot a single dart straight up at whoever or whatever stepped on the plate. The trap makes a ranged attack at +8, inflicting 1d4 piercing damage. The darts are covered with Oil of Taggit, requiring a DC 13 Constitution save for the creature not to fall unconscious for 24 hours or until damaged.

B. Legbite Snapjaws: An area of the floor here is a pressure plate that drops down. Strong, toothed metal "shoes" then snap out from under the edges of the adjacent floor, inflicting 1d4 bludgeoning damage on ankles (or other limbs) caught in them and inflicting the **restrained** condition. A successful DC 14 Dexterity save avoids taking damage and being restrained. A successful DC 16 Strength check is necessary to free a victim.

C. Locking Pit: A hidden, 10-foot-deep (1d6 falling damage) pit trap with a spring-loaded trap door that snaps shut over anyone falling in. A DC 16 Dexterity save avoids falling. A successful DC 20 Strength check can pry the cover open, or it can be smashed open (AC 17, 33 hp). It cannot be "disabled" to open, even from within the pit.

D. Falling Block: An area of the floor here is a pressure plate that drops down, triggering a stone block to plummet from the ceiling with a rattle of chains. It slams down to deal either 1d10 bludgeoning damage from a solid hit, or only a glancing blow of 1 damage on a successful DC 15 Dexterity saving throw. The block is immediately drawn back up into the ceiling by the mechanism above, and can be triggered to fall again.

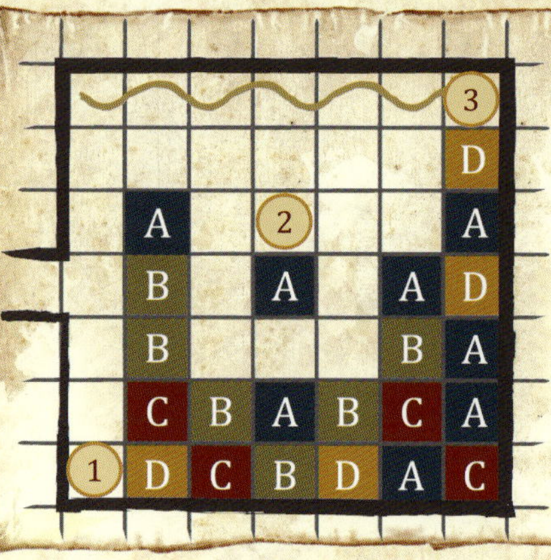

Ritual Room

1. Stairs
2. Altar
3. Curtains

Qeldra's Entrance

Waiting silently behind the curtains here is a slender woman in black leather armor, complete with a metal gorget, metal anklets over her boots (where her breeches end), and black leather elbow-length gauntlets. Her head is unprotected. She has waist-length, heavy, arrow-straight jet-black hair oiled so that it gleams, and it moves in a single tress. Her skin is the hue of birchwood, her eyes are large, intent, and amber-hued under heavy, commanding black brows, and her nose is tiny, pointed, and upswept at its tip, giving her a mischievous expression. She walks with lithe grace (and is a consummate actress).

This is **Qeldra**, leader of the brigands who work with the Horoth, and a skilled recruiter for her fictitious dragon cult thanks to good acting abilities, shrewd judgments of human character, and much practice. From behind the curtains, she'll listen to the PCs as they enter the room and look about, so as to learn as much as she can about their intentions and capabilities. She will step out through the curtains to confront them if they start to vandalize, are about to discover her, or begin to depart the room.

Qeldra will try to awe PCs with her claims of the numerical strength (hundreds of members) and great influence (in the form of behind-the-throne schemers) of the cult. She will try to recruit them to be a strike force for the cult, promising 50 gp a month to each PC, in addition to allowing them to keep any "loot" they gain. She will (falsely) tell the PCs that:

"We, the followers of the wise and benevolent Eirderreth, who do the sometimes nasty things that are necessary to get the right things done, worship Eirderreth so that he will continue to manifest from beyond the grave to guide us. Eirderreth sees a future of prosperity for people who follow his guidance, curbing cruel rulers and those who oppress and pursue greedy ends. He works towards a better future for all people of good will, in balance with the land, pursing the eradication of orcs, trolls, ogres, and others who despoil and slay wantonly. Throw your lot in with us, adventurers, and enjoy the guidance of the Dead Dragon and the support and aid that we, his faithful, will provide! Stand against us, and it shall be my reluctant duty to oppose you!"

If the PCs agree to work with the cult, Qeldra will assign them an expeditionary adventure of the leader's choice, sending them off elsewhere into danger. If they ask for time to consider her offer, Qeldra will politely bid them farewell and let them go, to face the challenges elsewhere in the Keep. If they attack her, Qeldra will fight them with her spells and mace. She knows the traps in this room very well, and will position herself to lure attacking PCs into them.

Qeldra

Medium humanoid (human), chaotic evil
- Armor Class 13 (leather armor)
- Hit Points 63 (14d8) | **Wound threshold** 16
- Speed 30 ft.

STR	DEX	CON	INT	WIS	CHA
9 (-1)	14 (+2)	11 (+0)	16 (+3)	18 (+4)	16 (+3)

- **Saving Throws** Wis +7
- **Skills** Arcana +6, Deception +6, Insight +7, Perception +7, Religion +6
- **Senses** passive Perception 17
- **Languages** Common, Draconic
- **Challenge** 5 (1,800 XP)

Special equipment. In addition to her *mace of paralysis*, Qeldra is equipped with: a *ring of mind shielding*; a spell scroll of *raise dead* (in a bone tube down her left boot); a dagger (tucked in her right boot); and two *potions of greater healing* (steel vials strapped to her belt in carry-thongs, which ride under her breeches; each vial restores 4d4+4 lost hp).

Spellcasting. Qeldra is a 7th-level spellcaster. Her spellcasting ability is Wisdom (spell save DC 15, +7 to hit with spell attacks). Qeldra has the following cleric spells prepared:
- Cantrips (at will): *light, mending, sacred flame, thaumaturgy*
- 1st level (4 slots): *cure wounds, guiding bolt, protection from evil and good, sanctuary*
- 2nd level (3 slots): *blindness/deafness, hold person, protection from poison*
- 3rd level (3 slots): *bestow curse, remove curse, speak with dead*
- 4th level (1 slot): *freedom of movement*

Actions

Multiattack. Qeldra makes two attacks with her *mace of paralysis* or dagger.
Dagger. *Melee Weapon Attack:* +5 to hit, reach 5 ft., one target. *Hit:* 4 (1d4+2) piercing damage.
Mace of paralysis. *Melee Weapon Attack:* +2 to hit, reach 5 ft., one target. *Hit:* 2 (1d6-1) bludgeoning damage. This is a metal one-piece weapon that does the usual mace damage, plus, upon a successful hit and at the expenditure of a charge, the effects of a *wand of paralysis*. It has 7 charges when the PCs encounter her. When fighting multiple foes, Qeldra rarely kills **paralyzed** foes, instead ignoring them to deal with those still active.

Who is Qeldra, Truly?

Qeldra's identity and background depend on what the leader wants to happen after this adventure. Her holy symbol, journal, or correspondence can serve as convenient plot hooks.

- **Priestess of a dead god.** Should the leader feature the Orb of Illusions in this adventure, Qeldra may have become a priestess following a sort of epiphany in the ancient ruins. Since then, she has been serving a bygone neutral or evil deity wishing to come back into existence. She has no clear indication of how she is supposed to achieve this, and has been groping for answers, looking for power, riches, and knowledge. The PCs will find a strange holy symbol on her. Should one of them keep it (to identify it, for example), the PC might receive strange dream visions from the deity, who will offer them powers in exchange for their service.

- **Priestess of Tamerakh.** The Destroyer appreciates how creative, power-hungry individuals can sow chaos. If the leader chooses this option, Qeldra can be an adept trained in Cyrillane, a country torn by civil war and by the havoc wreaked by sects worshiping evil divinities. Before she became the leader of the sect, seeking power and riches through her association with the Horoth, Qeldra may have been encouraged by her peers to upset the Free City and the surrounding lands.

- **Priestess of Xonim.** The Lady of the Night is a goddess of complex schemes and serpentine interventions. Ambitious characters sometimes draw her attention, as the many obstacles and betrayals they inevitably meet distract her. Her intent may also have been to undermine the influence of the draconic cults, which she seems to regard with enmity. This option restricts the possibility of a more overarching arc, which can be fitting if the leader wishes for the plot to be limited to this adventure only.

- **A victim of the Horoth.** Whatever option the leader picks, Qeldra could also be the first victim of the Horoth, slowly losing her mind while being convinced that she must associate with the monster, maybe even serve it, as a larval Horoth grows inside her head. This infestation may have occurred when she investigated the place in which the Horoth had been imprisoned and freed it. The Horoth may also have used Qeldra's interest in unusual phenomena to lure her into its service and turn her into a useful thrall. If the leader picks this option, triumphant PCs may see a worm slither out of Qeldra's fallen body, which will also be a way to let them know of the Horoth's plans. Such a horrific sight requires a successful DC 14 Wisdom save not to suffer from short-term madness.

Large Cellar

A large, dank, storage room lined with stone blocks, 60 feet east-west and 90 feet north-south, with a row of stout stone support columns down its center, and a ceiling 20 feet up. There, two cultists (see the entries for the Entry Hall and the Guardroom) are stationed, making use of the many small spyholes in the ceiling to direct the castle's defenses against the intruding PCs.
These cultists are **thugs** armed with maces and daggers.
Along the west wall of this room are a row of twelve crude wooden cots, with sleeping furs atop them and (thankfully empty) chamber pots underneath each. There is also one stout wooden bench and table at the north end of the row. Asleep on one of the cots is Glyve, a pet rat that will scurry away from the PCs, then towards PCs, then wildly everywhere. It is half-blind and toothless, only able to suck and not bite (no damage), but its erratic movements and speed give it an AC of 20. The leader should play it for humor, letting it jump inside PCs' clothing and gear, run along PC weapons, cling across PC faces as it voids itself in fear, and so on. Glyve has 2 hp. If killed by a PC, its tiny body will burst to splat out something it swallowed: a gleaming, faceted green gem (emerald) worth 2000 gp.

Oubliette

This 20-foot-by-30-foot stone-lined room is dark and reeks of rotting garbage and human waste. The stench arises from a central 10-foot-diameter shaft surrounded by a 3-foot-high stone wall that was formerly the Keep well, until it dried up. Ever since, the 100-foot-deep shaft has been used as a refuse pit, and the bottom thirty feet of it are now full of packed, unyielding waste, with another ten feet of wet, spongy, slimy sewage atop that.
The reek arising from the open-topped shaft is chokingly strong and bad. The room also contains a pair of mummified bare feet, severed at the ankle and previously belonging to a male human. The rest of the body formerly attached to them is missing, probably fed to the Horoth long ago. There is also a simple wooden three-legged stool. If a PC turns it over or examines it carefully, they will find 6 gold coins stuck to its underside with a thick, still strongly adhesive plant-sap goo.
Down in the pit, some ambulatory fungi live in the liquid waste, feeding off it. They are mindless, but will stir when light and sounds reach them, causing the bottom of the pit to bubble and move with wet sucking and flowing sounds, as if a submerged monster is stirring. These fungi consist of a morel-like, irregular, mottled brown fissured body dragged along by a brown slug-like tentacle. Disturbed fungi will thrust their tentacles up out of the muck to writhe and slap the shaft walls and surface of the muck, as if a large and energetic tentacled monster is emerging.
There is in fact no menace to the PCs here, and no monster to fight. Fishing around in the reeking muck won't turn up anything of value except a corroded but still sturdy crowbar and a greatsword in the same condition, its scabbard rotted away.

If this adventure is to be played as part of a campaign, this is an ideal place to have the PCs discover a submerged skeleton carrying a map and/or cryptic message, keys, or a token of some sort leading to future adventures elsewhere. To expand the Keep, it will be easy to add secret doors opening to lower levels that roll open by themselves when a PC carrying a token found on the aforementioned skeleton approaches.

Deep Cellar

In this deepest room of the Keep (its former treasury) reposes the Horoth, a rare sort of sapient creature that is in league with the brigands who have concocted this false cult. The Horoth sees the cult as a way to expand its influence by getting people to serve it, as it poses as "the Voice of Eirderreth."
PCs arriving in the Deep Cellar will see a 50-foot-square, 20-foot-high room with a ceiling glowing a gentle amber. The light is from a *faerie fire* spell and is meant for purely aesthetic purposes, as the Horoth doesn't need it to see. Across the back of the room, zig-zagging about 10 feet away from the wall in the central 30 feet of the room, is a 10-foot-high lacquered wooden ornamental screen, its bottom flush with the floor and with flaring "feet" at every hinge. Its base hue is glossy black, and atop that has been painted fantastic images of flying, snarling dragons blowing gouts of bright flame at each other as they soar and whirl.
Out in front of the screen is a sturdy, heavy table made of four squat blocks of stone with a thick slab of granite atop them. It weighs almost a ton, and so is immobile without destructive force or all of the PCs straining together to shift it. It is stained and spattered with old blood... lots of old blood. The Horoth eats its meals raw, off of the table.
There is no meal on the table now. Instead, the Horoth has arranged its weapons at the ready there: two greataxes and two unsheathed greatswords, ready for use. As soon as the PCs enter, before any of them can reach the table or the weapons on it, the Horoth will glide into view from behind the screen and position itself behind the table where it can readily reach the weapons as it speaks to the PCs.

Chests and Traps

Arranged around the walls of the room are 12 large (4-foot-high, 3-foot-wide, 5-foot-long) hoop-topped, brassbound wooden chests, "pirate treasure chests" in style.

Itself immune to poison, the Horoth surrounds itself with these, for they are all empty, unlocked traps intended for intruders. Lifting the lid of any treasure chest shoots out a trio of poisoned darts. Each dart makes a +8 bonus ranged attack against a random target within 10 feet. If no one is within range, the darts harmlessly ricochet off the ceiling, breaking their poison tips into useless powder when they hit. A successful hit deals 1d4 piercing damage and forces a DC 15 Constitution saving throw, causing 1d10 poison damage if successful, 2d10 if failed. Each chest "reloads" itself once if the lid falls closed again, so each can fire two volleys of three poisoned darts.

Around the chests are heaped piles of hundreds of "gold coins" that are all just gold-painted wooden discs. These are tokens used as money within the cult, but to the PCs and other non-cultists, they will seem merely like sham money.

Anatomy of the Horoth

The Horoth is a large, fat snake with a darker scaled back and sides, and a lighter scaled underbelly, like a naga. Its back scales are chestnut-brown and gleaming, and its underbelly is maroon around the edges, fading to light green in the center. Its muscular serpentine torso ripples when active and has a stinger tail at one end. The other end culminates in a horned head shaped like the head of a horse, only with fanged jaws.

In a fringe around and just below this head, the Horoth has four human-like arms that are as dexterous and as capable of precise motor activities as a skilled and strong adult human. They are also large and strong enough to each wield a polearm or oversized weapon (for example, a sword considered "two-handed" for a medium creature) without penalty. Their spacing and full-swivel shoulder joints means they don't normally "get in each other's way."

The Horoth's pale purple tongue is retractable and over 3 feet long, forked, sticky, and prehensile; it can lick itself clean with ease and use its tongue to open locks and slides, and pick up keys, coins, and other small objects.

Meeting the Horoth

If the PCs speak with the Horoth rather than merely attacking or fleeing, it will introduce itself as the voice of Eirderreth, and pose as a kindly, helpful being who likes making new friends and meeting new people in general. It will offer the PCs places in the cult and a mission: to find and bring back to it the human named Avrath Hondolym, a "vile criminal" who has "worked dark rituals" that the "Faithful of Eirderreth" must know much more about so that they can undo these dark magics (which have something to do with "sickening babies as yet unborn, and reducing the minds and wills of people until they become as worms").

This is all false, of course. In truth, the Horoth is a ruthless, calculating predator that eats people and any other raw meat it can get.

The Horoth's Screen

The Horoth's screen may look as if it can be tipped over, but at each hinged joint, there's a pin between the stabilizing feet that runs down into a hole in the stone floor of this room, holding the screen solidly in place. It will have to be lifted in sections (a PC at either end of the same section lifting in unison) to move it, or chopped through with weapons. It's far more likely that PCs will simply race around either end of it, once they discover how solidly anchored it is.

Behind the screen is a long, deep heap of soft pillows that serve the Horoth as a bed. Each one is subtly different, and in the damp, most of them have begun to mildew on their undersides. One of them, at the bottom of the heap, has an open bit of seam just big enough to fit a small wooden coffer containing 86 gp, and a small, hinged brass box holding four faceted rubies worth 3000 gp each, individually wrapped in silk to keep them from being marred, buried deep within the heart of the pillow.

Horoth

Large monstrosity, chaotic evil

- **Armor Class** 15 (natural armor)
- **Hit Points** 75 (10d10+20) | **Wound threshold** 19
- **Speed** 40 ft.

STR	DEX	CON	INT	WIS	CHA
18 (+4)	17 (+3)	14 (+2)	16 (+3)	15 (+2)	16 (+3)

- **Saving Throws** Dex +6, Con +5, Wis +5, Cha +6
- **Damage Immunities** poison
- **Condition Immunities** charmed, poisoned
- **Senses** darkvision 60 ft., passive Perception 12
- **Languages** Common, Draconic
- **Challenge** 5 (1,800 XP)

Perpetual faerie fire. The Horoth can cast *faerie fire* at will.
Dementing saliva. The Horoth can produce a saliva-like substance that is mixed with wine and shared between the members of the cult in the course of their draconic ceremonies. Its effect only triggers when the imbiber suffers from intense stress, for example under the fear of having been captured, in which case they fall into a state of confusion that will last 4d6 hours.

Actions

Multiattack. The Horoth makes up to 6 attacks: a bite attack, 4 weapon and/or claw attacks, and a sting with its tail.
Bite. *Melee Weapon Attack:* +7 to hit, reach 5 ft., one target. *Hit:* 7 (1d6 + 4) piercing damage.
Claws. *Melee Weapon Attack:* +7 to hit, reach 5 ft., one target. *Hit:* 7 (1d6 + 4) piercing damage.
Greataxe. *Melee Weapon Attack:* +7 to hit, reach 5 ft., one target. *Hit:* 10 (1d12 + 4) slashing damage.
Greatsword. *Melee Weapon Attack:* +7 to hit, reach 5 ft., one target. *Hit:* 11 (2d6 + 4) slashing damage.
Tail Sting. *Melee Weapon Attack:* +7 to hit, reach 5 ft., one target. *Hit:* 7 (1d6 + 4) piercing damage plus target must make a DC 13 Constitution saving throw, taking 10 (3d6) poison damage on a failed save, or half as much damage on a successful one.

Fighting the Horoth

The Horoth's usual tactics are to disable spellcasters first and move about striking at foes and moving on, trying to get foes to stumble into each other's way. It likes to deal damage and move about ceaselessly, and will only stay to batter a single target if it thinks other foes are puny or disabled. It will be acutely aware of spellcasters needing to concentrate to maintain their spells, and will therefore endeavor to disrupt them.

If the battle goes against the Horoth, it will back behind the screen, seeking to lure the PCs into attacking it from one direction, using its tail to heap up the pillows behind it into a hampering, moving barrier that the Horoth will plunge under and through if pressed, leaving most of the PCs on the other side.

The Legend of the Horoth

The Horoth is a rare creature that the PCs may know about with a successful DC 20 Intelligence (Arcana or History) check. The leader may also conveniently include information about the monster in Qeldra's journal. At the leader's discretion, its story may lead to a full-fledged campaign or end with this adventure.

- **Freed from ruins.** Qeldra discovered the Horoth in a state of stasis, inside a prison in the heart of a Traveler ruin. Being regarded as too dangerous, the monster was confined there, probably for study. The proliferation of those bearing the Horoth's spawn would be disastrous. Would the PCs manage to curb this threat, even if it means waging war on an entire evil species?

- **Exotic peril.** The Horoth ordinarily inhabits warm, sunny lands, such as the jungles of the Ajagar or the deserts of Ghardat. However, as misfortune had it, an infested wizard was subsequently enslaved and taken to the land of the Free City. The spawn eventually matured, killing its host, and sought to spread its kin in this less hospitable region. But with the swift, decisive action of the PCs and the deaths of the previously kidnapped persons, these dreadful projects never come to pass.

If the Horoth is losing the battle, it will try to fight its way out of the Deep Cellar and plunge down the Oubliette and into its wet goo, wriggling down through it to a hidden refuge side chamber below that is free of refuse and has breathable air. There, it will wait for a day or more, in hopes that the PCs will depart. It has a cache of six *potions of superior healing* (each steel vial restores 8d4+8 lost hp) in this refuge and will use them if sorely wounded.

After the Adventure

Although the cult is a sham and "Dead Dragon Keep" is a local nickname, there is a dragon's ghost haunting the ruined castle. It will take an interest in the PCs and follow surviving PCs wherever they go, whispering to them in their dreams—and sometimes, in moments of extreme peril or indecision—for the rest of their lives, "adopting" them as something akin to pets it wants to see succeed and is entertained by. The ghost will be reluctant to reveal its name or true nature, so the leader should make learning such things a long process, possibly requiring the PCs to be deceptive and quick-witted.

Appendix

Bandit

Medium humanoid (any race), any non-lawful alignment
- **Armor Class** 12 (leather armor)
- **Hit Points** 11 (2d8+2) | **Wound threshold** 5
- **Speed** 30 ft.

STR	DEX	CON	INT	WIS	CHA
11 (+0)	12 (+1)	12 (+1)	10 (+0)	10 (+0)	10 (+0)

- **Senses** passive Perception 10
- **Languages** any one language (usually Common)
- **Challenge** 1/8 (25 XP)

Actions

Scimitar. *Melee Weapon Attack:* +3 to hit, reach 5 ft., one target. *Hit:* 4 (1d6 + 1) slashing damage.
Light Crossbow. *Ranged Weapon Attack:* +3 to hit, reach 80/320 ft., one target. *Hit:* 5 (1d8 + 1) piercing damage.

Dire Wolf

Large beast, unaligned
- **Armor Class** 14 (natural armor)
- **Hit Points** 37 (5d10+10) | **Wound threshold** 10
- **Speed** 50 ft.

STR	DEX	CON	INT	WIS	CHA
17 (+3)	15 (+2)	15 (+2)	6 (-2)	12 (+1)	10 (+0)

- **Skills** Perception +3, Stealth +4
- **Senses** passive Perception 13
- **Languages** —
- **Challenge** 1 (200 XP)

Keen Hearing and Smell. The wolf has advantage on Wisdom (Perception) checks that rely on hearing or smell.
Pack Tactics. The wolf has advantage on an attack roll against a creature if at least one of the wolf's allies is within 5 ft. of the creature and the ally isn't incapacitated.

Actions

Bite. *Melee Weapon Attack:* +5 to hit, reach 5 ft., one target. *Hit:* 10 (2d6 + 3) piercing damage. If the target is a creature, it must succeed on a DC 13 Strength saving throw or be knocked **prone**.

Draft Horse

Large beast, unaligned
- **Armor Class** 10
- **Hit Points** 19 (3d10+3) | **Wound threshold** 5
- **Speed** 40 ft.

STR	DEX	CON	INT	WIS	CHA
18 (+4)	10 (+0)	12 (+1)	4 (-3)	11 (+0)	7 (-2)

- **Senses** passive Perception 10
- **Languages** —
- **Challenge** 1/4 (50 XP)

Actions

Hooves. *Melee Weapon Attack:* +6 to hit, reach 5 ft., one target. *Hit:* 9 (2d4 + 4) bludgeoning damage.

Ettercap

Medium monstrosity, neutral evil

- **Armor Class** 13 (natural armor)
- **Hit Points** 44 (8d8+8) | **Wound threshold** 11
- **Speed** 30 ft., climb 30 ft.

STR	DEX	CON	INT	WIS	CHA
14 (+2)	15 (+2)	13 (+1)	7 (-2)	12 (+1)	8 (-1)

- **Skills** Perception +3, Stealth +4, Survival +3
- **Senses** darkvision 60 ft., passive Perception 13
- **Languages** —
- **Challenge** 2 (450 XP)

Spider Climb. The ettercap can climb difficult surfaces, including upside down on ceilings, without needing to make an ability check.
Web Sense. While in contact with a web, the ettercap knows the exact location of any other creature in contact with the same web.
Web Walker. The ettercap ignores movement restrictions caused by webbing.

Actions

Multiattack. The ettercap makes two attacks: one with its bite and one with its claws.
Bite. *Melee Weapon Attack:* +4 to hit, reach 5 ft., one creature. *Hit:* 6 (1d8 + 2) piercing damage plus (1d8) poison damage. The target must succeed on a DC 11 Constitution saving throw or be **poisoned** for 1 minute. The creature can repeat the saving throw at the end of each of its turns, ending the effect on itself on a success.
Claws. *Melee Weapon Attack:* +4 to hit, reach 5 ft., one target. *Hit:* 7 (2d4 + 2) slashing damage.
Web (Recharge 5-6). *Ranged Weapon Attack:* +4 to hit, reach 30/60 ft., one large or smaller creature. The creature is **restrained** by webbing. As an action, the restrained creature can make a DC 11 Strength check, escaping from the webbing on a success. The effect ends if the webbing is destroyed. The webbing has AC 10, 5 hit points, resistance to bludgeoning damage, and immunity to poison and psychic damage.

Ettin

Large giant, chaotic evil

- **Armor Class** 12 (natural armor)
- **Hit Points** 85 (10d10+30) | **Wound threshold** 22
- **Speed** 40 ft.

STR	DEX	CON	INT	WIS	CHA
21 (+5)	8 (-1)	17 (+3)	6 (-2)	10 (+0)	8 (-1)

- **Skills** Perception +4
- **Senses** darkvision 60 ft., passive Perception 14
- **Languages** Giant, Orc
- **Challenge** 4 (1,100 XP)

Two Heads. The ettin has advantage on Wisdom (Perception) checks and on saving throws against being blinded, charmed, deafened, frightened, stunned, and knocked unconscious.
Wakeful. When one of the ettin's heads is asleep, its other head is awake.

Actions

Multiattack. The ettin makes two attacks: one with its battleaxe and one with its morningstar.
Battleaxe. *Melee Weapon Attack:* +7 to hit, reach 5 ft., one target. *Hit:* 14 (2d8 + 5) slashing damage.
Morningstar. *Melee Weapon Attack:* +7 to hit, reach 5 ft., one target. *Hit:* 14 (2d8 + 5) piercing damage.

Giant Spider

Large beast, unaligned
- **Armor Class** 14 (natural armor)
- **Hit Points** 26 (4d10+4) | **Wound threshold** 7
- **Speed** 30 ft., climb 30 ft.

STR	DEX	CON	INT	WIS	CHA
14 (+2)	16 (+3)	12 (+1)	2 (-4)	11 (0)	4 (-3)

- **Skills** Stealth +7
- **Senses** blindsight 10 ft., darkvision 60 ft., passive Perception 10
- **Languages** —
- **Challenge** 1 (200 XP)

Spider Climb. The spider can climb difficult surfaces, including upside down on ceilings, without needing to make an ability check.
Web Sense. While in contact with a web, the spider knows the exact location of any other creature in contact with the same web.
Web Walker. The spider ignores movement restrictions caused by webbing.

Actions

Bite. *Melee Weapon Attack:* +5 to hit, reach 5 ft., one creature. *Hit:* 7 (1d8 + 3) piercing damage, and the target must make a DC 11 Constitution saving throw, taking 9 (2d8) poison damage on a failed save, or half as much damage on a successful one. If the poison damage reduces the target to 0 hit points, the target is stable but **poisoned** for 1 hour, even after regaining hit points, and is **paralyzed** while poisoned in this way.
Web (Recharge 5-6). *Ranged Weapon Attack:* +5 to hit, reach 30/60 ft., one creature. The target is **restrained** by webbing. As an action, the restrained target can make a DC 12 Strength check, bursting the webbing on a success. The webbing can also be attacked and destroyed (AC 10; hp 5; vulnerability to fire damage; immunity to bludgeoning, poison, and psychic damage).

Hell Hound

Medium fiend, lawful evil
- **Armor Class** 15 (natural armor)
- **Hit Points** 45 (7d8+14) | **Wound threshold** 12
- **Speed** 50 ft.

STR	DEX	CON	INT	WIS	CHA
17 (+3)	12 (+1)	14 (+2)	6 (-2)	13 (+1)	6 (-2)

- **Skills** Perception +5
- **Damage Immunities** Fire
- **Senses** darkvision 60 ft., passive Perception 12
- **Languages** understands Infernal but can't speak it
- **Challenge** 3 (700 XP)

Keen Hearing and Smell. The hound has advantage on Wisdom (Perception) checks that rely on hearing or smell.

Pack Tactics. The hound has advantage on an attack roll against a creature if at least one of the hound's allies is within 5 ft. of the creature and the ally isn't incapacitated.

Actions

Bite. *Melee Weapon Attack:* +5 to hit, reach 5 ft., one target. *Hit:* 7 (1d8 + 3) piercing damage plus 7 (2d6) fire damage.
Fire Breath (Recharge 5-6). The hound exhales fire in a 15-foot cone. Each creature in that area must make a DC 12 Dexterity saving throw, taking 21 (6d6) fire damage on a failed save, or half as much damage on a successful one.

Manticore (Aging)

Large monstrosity, lawful evil
- **Armor Class** 14 (natural armor)
- **Hit Points** 44 | **Wound threshold** 11
- **Speed** 30 ft.

STR	DEX	CON	INT	WIS	CHA
17 (+3)	16 (+3)	17 (+3)	7 (-2)	12 (+1)	8 (-1)

- **Senses** darkvision 60 ft., passive Perception 11
- **Languages** —
- **Challenge** 3 (700 XP)

Tail Spike Regrowth. The manticore has three tail spikes. Used spikes regrow when the manticore has finished three long rests.

Actions

Multiattack. The manticore makes three attacks: one with its bite and two with its claws or three with its tail spikes.
Bite. *Melee Weapon Attack:* +5 to hit, reach 5 ft., one target. *Hit:* 7 (1d8 + 3) piercing damage.
Claw. *Melee Weapon Attack:* +5 to hit, reach 5 ft., one target. *Hit:* 6 (1d6 + 3) slashing damage.
Tail Spike. *Ranged Weapon Attack:* +5 to hit, reach 100/200 ft., one target. *Hit:* 7 (1d8 + 3) piercing damage.

Minotaur

Large monstrosity, chaotic evil
- **Armor Class** 14 (natural armor)
- **Hit Points** 76 (9d10+27) | **Wound threshold** 19
- **Speed** 40 ft.

STR	DEX	CON	INT	WIS	CHA
18 (+4)	11 (+0)	16 (+3)	6 (-2)	16 (+3)	9 (-1)

- **Skills** Perception +7
- **Senses** darkvision 60 ft., passive Perception 17
- **Languages** Abyssal
- **Challenge** 3 (700 XP)

Charge. If the minotaur moves at least 10 ft. straight toward a target and then hits it with a gore attack on the same turn, the target takes an extra 9 (2d8) piercing damage. If the target is a creature, it must succeed on a DC 14 Strength saving throw or be pushed up to 10 ft. away and knocked prone.

Labyrinthine Recall. The minotaur can perfectly recall any path it has traveled.

Reckless. At the start of its turn, the minotaur can gain advantage on all melee weapon attack rolls it makes during that turn, but attack rolls against it have advantage until the start of its next turn.

Actions

Greataxe. *Melee Weapon Attack:* +6 to hit, reach 5 ft., one target. *Hit:* 17 (2d12 + 4) slashing damage.

Gore. *Melee Weapon Attack:* +6 to hit, reach 5 ft., one target. *Hit:* 13 (2d8 + 4) piercing damage.

Owlbear

Large monstrosity, unaligned
- **Armor Class** 13 (natural armor)
- **Hit Points** 59 (7d10+21) | **Wound threshold** 15
- **Speed** 40 ft.

STR	DEX	CON	INT	WIS	CHA
20 (+5)	12 (+1)	17 (+3)	3 (-4)	12 (+1)	7 (-2)

- **Skills** Perception +3
- **Senses** darkvision 60 ft., passive Perception 13
- **Challenge** 3 (700 XP)

Keen Sight and Smell. The owlbear has advantage on Wisdom (Perception) checks that rely on sight or smell.

Actions

Multiattack. The owlbear makes two attacks: one with its beak and one with its claws.

Beak. *Melee Weapon Attack:* +7 to hit, reach 5 ft., one creature. *Hit:* 10 (1d10 + 5) piercing damage.

Claws. *Melee Weapon Attack:* +7 to hit, reach 5 ft., one target. *Hit:* 14 (2d8 + 5) slashing damage.

Scout

Medium humanoid (any race), any alignment
- **Armor Class** 13 (leather armor)
- **Hit Points** 16 (3d8+3) | **Wound threshold** 5
- **Speed** 30 ft.

STR	DEX	CON	INT	WIS	CHA
11 (+0)	14 (+2)	12 (+1)	11 (+0)	13 (+1)	11 (+0)

- **Skills** Nature +4, Perception +5, Stealth +6, Survival +5
- **Senses** passive Perception 15
- **Languages** any one language (usually Common)
- **Challenge** 1/2 (100 XP)

Keen Hearing and Sight. The scout has advantage on Wisdom (Perception) checks that rely on hearing or sight.

Actions

Multiattack. The scout makes two melee attacks or two ranged attacks.

Shortsword. *Melee Weapon Attack:* +4 to hit, reach 5 ft., one target. *Hit:* 5 (1d6 + 2) piercing damage.

Longbow. *Ranged Weapon Attack:* +4 to hit, reach 150/600 ft., one target. *Hit:* 6 (1d8 + 2) piercing damage.

Stirge

Tiny beast, unaligned
- **Armor Class** 14 (natural armor)
- **Hit Points** 2 (1d4) | **Wound threshold** N/A
- **Speed** 10 ft., fly 40 ft.

STR	DEX	CON	INT	WIS	CHA
4 (-3)	16 (+3)	11 (+0)	2 (-4)	8 (-1)	6 (-2)

- **Senses** darkvision 60 ft., passive Perception 9
- **Languages** —
- **Challenge** 1/8 (25 XP)

Actions

Blood Drain. *Melee Weapon Attack:* +5 to hit, reach 5 ft., one creature. *Hit:* 5 (1d4 + 3) piercing damage. The stirge attaches to the target. While attached, the stirge doesn't attack. Instead, at the start of each of the stirge's turns, the target loses 5 (1d4 + 3) hit points due to blood loss.
The stirge can detach itself by spending 5 feet of its movement. It does so after it drains 10 hit points of blood from the target or the target dies. A creature, including the target, can use its action to detach the stirge.

Swarm of Poisonous Snakes

Medium swarm of Tiny beasts, unaligned
- **Armor Class** 14
- **Hit Points** 36 (8d8) | **Wound threshold** N/A
- **Speed** 30 ft., swim 30 ft.

STR	DEX	CON	INT	WIS	CHA
8 (-1)	18 (+4)	11 (+0)	1 (-5)	10 (+0)	3 (-4)

- **Damage Resistance** bludgeoning, piercing, slashing
- **Condition Immunities** charmed, frightened, grappled, paralyzed, petrified, prone, restrained, stunned
- **Senses** blindsight 10 ft., passive Perception 10
- **Languages** —
- **Challenge** 2 (450 XP)

Swarm. The swarm can occupy another creature's space and vice versa, and the swarm can move through any opening large enough for a Tiny snake. The swarm can't regain hit points or gain temporary hit points.

Actions

Bites. *Melee Weapon Attack:* +6 to hit, reach 0 ft., one creature in the swarm's space. *Hit:* 7 (2d6) piercing damage, or 3 (1d6) piercing damage if the swarm has half of its hit points or fewer. The target must make a DC 10 Constitution saving throw, taking 14 (4d6) poison damage on a failed save, or half as much damage on a successful one.

Thug

Medium humanoid (any race), any non-good alignment
- **Armor Class** 11 (leather armor)
- **Hit Points** 32 (5d8+10) | **Wound threshold** 8
- **Speed** 30 ft.

STR	DEX	CON	INT	WIS	CHA
15 (+2)	11 (+0)	14 (+2)	10 (+0)	10 (+0)	11 (+0)

- **Skills** Intimidation +2
- **Senses** passive Perception 10
- **Languages** any one language (usually Common)
- **Challenge** 1/2 (100 XP)

Pack Tactics. The thug has advantage on an attack roll against a creature if at least one of the thug's allies is within 5 ft. of the creature and the ally isn't incapacitated.

Actions

Multiattack. The thug makes two melee attacks.
Mace. *Melee Weapon Attack:* +4 to hit, reach 5 ft., one creature. *Hit:* 5 (1d6 + 2) bludgeoning damage.
Heavy Crossbow. *Ranged Weapon Attack:* +2 to hit, reach 100/400 ft., one target. *Hit:* 5 (1d10) piercing damage.

Veteran

Medium humanoid (any race), any alignment
• **Armor Class** 17 (splint)
• **Hit Points** 58 (9d8 + 18) | **Wound threshold** 15
• **Speed** 30 ft.

STR	DEX	CON	INT	WIS	CHA
16 (+3)	13 (+1)	14 (+2)	12 (+1)	12 (+1)	10 (+0)

• **Skills** Athletics +5, Perception +2
• **Senses** passive Perception 12
• **Languages** any one language (usually Common)
• **Challenge** 3 (700 XP)

Actions

Multiattack. The veteran makes two longsword attacks. If it has a shortsword drawn, it can also make a shortsword attack.
Longsword. *Melee Weapon Attack:* +5 to hit, reach 5 ft., one target. *Hit:* 7 (1d8 + 3) slashing damage, or 8 (1d10 + 3) slashing damage if used with two hands.
Shortsword. *Melee Weapon Attack:* +5 to hit, reach 5 ft., one target. *Hit:* 6 (1d6 + 3) piercing damage.
Heavy Crossbow. *Ranged Weapon Attack:* +3 to hit, range 100/400 ft., one target. *Hit:* 6 (1d10 + 1) piercing damage.

Warhorse

Large beast, unaligned
• **Armor Class** 11
• **Hit Points** 19 (3d10 + 3) | **Wound threshold** 5
• **Speed** 60 ft.

STR	DEX	CON	INT	WIS	CHA
18 (+4)	12 (+1)	13 (+1)	4 (-3)	12 (+1)	7 (-2)

• **Senses** passive Perception 11
• **Languages** —
• **Challenge** 1/2 (100 XP)

Trampling Charge. If the horse moves at least 20 feet straight toward a creature and then hits it with a hooves attack on the same turn, that target must succeed on a DC 14 Strength saving throw or be knocked **prone**. If the target is prone, the horse can make another attack with its hooves against it as a bonus action.

Actions

Hooves. *Melee Weapon Attack:* +6 to hit, reach 5 ft., one target. *Hit:* 11 (2d6 + 4) bludgeoning damage.

Wolf

Medium beast, unaligned
• **Armor Class** 13 (natural armor)
• **Hit Points** 11 (2d8 + 2) | **Wound threshold** 5
• **Speed** 40 ft.

STR	DEX	CON	INT	WIS	CHA
12 (+1)	15 (+2)	12 (+1)	5 (-3)	12 (+1)	9 (-1)

• **Skills** Perception +3, Stealth +4
• **Senses** passive Perception 13
• **Languages** —
• **Challenge** 1/4 (50 XP)

Keen Hearing and Smell. The wolf has advantage on Wisdom (Perception) checks that rely on hearing or smell.
Pack Tactics. The wolf has advantage on attack rolls against a creature if at least one of the wolf's allies is within 5 feet of the creature and the ally isn't incapacitated.

Actions

Bite. *Melee Weapon Attack:* +4 to hit, reach 5 ft., one target. *Hit:* 7 (2d4 + 2) piercing damage. If the target is a creature, it must succeed on a DC 11 Strength saving throw or be knocked **prone**.

Discover the universe of Eana and its many unique civilizations, battle the loathsome forces of Canker, find the lost portals of the Travelers, and ascend the stairs of the Fateforge!

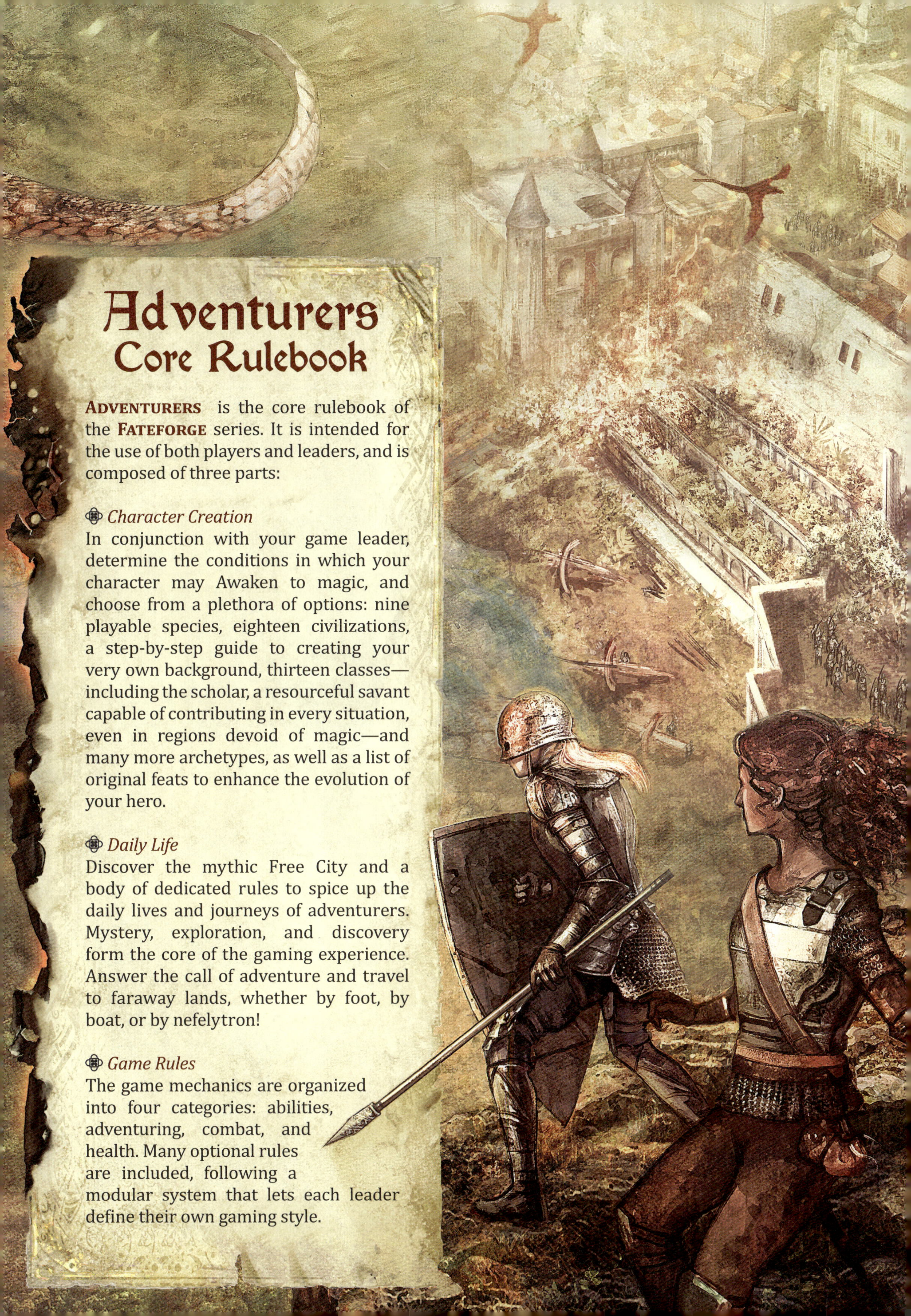

Adventurers
Core Rulebook

Adventurers is the core rulebook of the **Fateforge** series. It is intended for the use of both players and leaders, and is composed of three parts:

Character Creation
In conjunction with your game leader, determine the conditions in which your character may Awaken to magic, and choose from a plethora of options: nine playable species, eighteen civilizations, a step-by-step guide to creating your very own background, thirteen classes—including the scholar, a resourceful savant capable of contributing in every situation, even in regions devoid of magic—and many more archetypes, as well as a list of original feats to enhance the evolution of your hero.

Daily Life
Discover the mythic Free City and a body of dedicated rules to spice up the daily lives and journeys of adventurers. Mystery, exploration, and discovery form the core of the gaming experience. Answer the call of adventure and travel to faraway lands, whether by foot, by boat, or by nefelytron!

Game Rules
The game mechanics are organized into four categories: abilities, adventuring, combat, and health. Many optional rules are included, following a modular system that lets each leader define their own gaming style.